GP

ACO-9269

ACO-9269

MY PET

Rats & Mice

Honor Head

Photographs by
Jane Burton

RAINTREE
STECK-VAUGHN
RSVP PUBLISHERS

A Harcourt Company

Austin   New York
www.steck-vaughn.com

Published by Raintree Steck-Vaughn
Publishers, an imprint of Steck-Vaughn
Company.

Editors: Claire Edwards, Erik Greb
Art Director: Max Brinkmann
Designer: Rosamund Saunders
Illustrator: Pauline Bayne

Printed in Singapore

1 2 3 4 5 6 7 8 9 0 LB 03 02 01 00

**Library of Congress Cataloging-in-Publication
Data**

Head, Honor.
  Rats and mice/Honor Head; photographs
by Jane Burton.
    p. cm.—(My pet)
  Summary: Describes the physical
characteristics and habits of rats and mice
and tells how to care for them as pets.
  ISBN 0-7398-2889-4 (hardcover)
  ISBN 0-7398-3014-7 (softcover)
  1. Rats as pets—Juvenile literature.
  2. Mice as pets—Juvenile literature.
  [1. Rats as pets. 2. Mice as pets.
  3. Pets.] I. Burton, Jane, ill. II. Title.

SF459.R3 H43 2000
636.9'352—dc21
                              00–027049

Contents

Owning Your Own Pet   5

What Is a Mouse?   6

What Is a Rat?   8

Newborn Rats and Mice   10

Cages and Tanks   12

Making Your Pets Comfortable   14

Exercising Your Pets   16

Playing with Your Pets   18

Eating and Drinking   20

Cleaning Your Pets' Home   22

Handling Your Pets   24

Your Pets' Health   26

Keeping Your Pets Safe   28

Words to Remember   30

Index   31

Notes for Parents   32

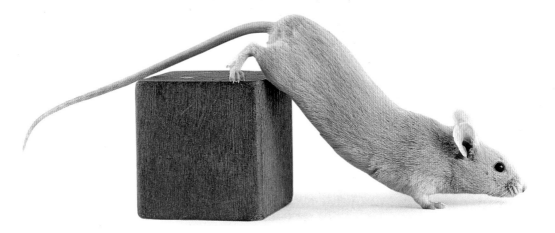

My Mouse

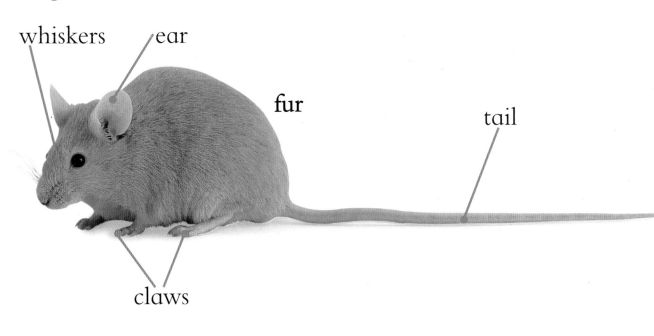

whiskers

ear

fur

tail

claws

My Rat

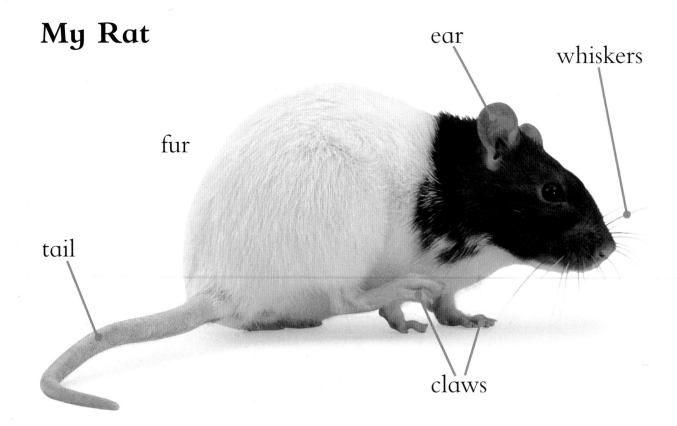

ear

whiskers

fur

tail

claws

It's fun to have your own pet.

Rats and mice are fun to own, but they need to be looked after carefully. Pet rats and mice have to be fed every day, and their home should be cleaned regularly. They need plenty of exercise, too, and should be handled daily.

Young children with pets should always work with an adult. For further notes, please see page 32.

What is a mouse?

Mice are part of the rodent family. They have a long tail and whiskers, and they make squeaking noises. You should keep more than one mouse. They like company.

Mice are all the same shape, but they come in lots of different colors.

Some mice are the same
color all over. Others
have stripes and
patches on
their fur.

Some mice have long fur.
But a mouse does not
have fur on its
feet, tail, or ears.

What is a rat?

Rats are also rodents. They are bigger than mice and have longer tails.

A rat's fur should be smooth and shiny. It should not have bare patches.

Rats come in different colors, such as brown, silver, and yellow. There are also albino rats. They are white and have pink eyes. Some rats have spots and stripes on their fur.

In the wild, rats live in big groups. You should always keep two or more pet rats together. Otherwise they will be lonely.

Rats and mice build nests for their babies.

Rats and mice prepare a nest for their babies. Make sure a pregnant female is well fed and has fresh water. She will need extra paper bedding, too, for making her nest.

Baby mice and rats are born without any fur. They cannot see or hear. Do not touch the babies for the first two weeks.

Rats can have as many as 16 babies. Mice may have up to 12, but they usually have litters of about 8 babies. The babies are ready to leave their mother when they are 5 to 6 weeks old.

Separate males and females when they are about five weeks old. If they are left together, they may have babies.

Make your pets a cozy home.

Your pets can live in a cage or a glass tank. A tank is the best home for a mouse. Make sure the tank or cage is big enough for your pets. This is very important if you are keeping two or more pets together.

Prepare your pets' home by covering the floor with wood shavings. Always buy the wood shavings from a pet store. Never use sawdust in your pet's home.

Your pets will also
need a cozy nest
to sleep in. Fill
a box with
shredded
paper bedding
material from
a pet store.

Do not keep rats and mice together in the same cage or tank.

13

Make sure your pets are comfortable.

Check that the tank or cage does not
have any plastic or wooden parts
that your pets can chew. Make sure
all the corners are smooth, so that
your pets cannot hurt themselves.

Give your pets plenty to chew on. This will help to make sure their teeth do not grow too long. You can buy special blocks of wood at the pet store for rats and mice to chew.

Mice and rats will be lonely if they are kept on their own. Keep females together. Males may fight. Don't put males and females in together. They will have a lot of unwanted babies.

A carrying container is useful when you take pets to the vet. You can also use it to keep pets safe when you clean out their home.

Your pets need lots of exercise.

Give your pets a wheel so that they can exercise. Make sure the wheel is solid, so your pet's tail or feet do not get caught.

Rats and mice are good climbers. They enjoy having a ladder or climbing frame they can run up and down on. A cube with holes in each side is fun for them to climb through.

Give your pets lots of things to play with. Try making a maze of bricks for them to explore. Do not give them toys made of soft plastic.

A simple cardboard tube makes an ideal toy for your pet rats and mice.

Your pets like to play.

Your pets will need to exercise outside the cage. But never let them run around the house by themselves. Always stay with your pets and make sure they are safe.

Your pets will enjoy playing with you. They like to run up and down your arm and sit on your shoulder. The more often you handle your rats, the friendlier they will become.

Rats have a good sense of balance and can climb along a rope hung in their cage.

Your pets love to explore. But watch them carefully, or they will chew any objects they find.

Give your pets fresh food every day.

Every day, give your pets
a bowl of food bought from
the pet store or vet. Put the
food in a heavy bowl, so that
your pets do not knock it over.

Foods such
as peanuts
and hard-
boiled eggs
are delicious
treats for
your pets.

Your pets will not drink very much, but make sure they always have a drip-feeder bottle full of fresh water.

Rats and mice enjoy fresh foods two or three times a week. Give them oats or millet, greens, carrots, and whole grain bread. Wash fruit and vegetables well. Do not feed your pets lettuce.

Keep your pets' cage clean.

It is important to keep your pets' home clean. This will keep them healthy and keep them from smelling. Clean out any old food and droppings every day. Wash the food bowl and make sure the water bottle is clean.

Once a week, clean out your pets' nesting box. Throw out the old stuff and put in some clean bedding material. Always wash your hands after cleaning your pets' home.

Mice and rats keep their fur very clean. They lick themselves all over several times a day.

Once a month, give your pets' home a thorough cleaning. Wash the cage or tank, toys, water bottle, and food bowls.

Make sure everything is dry before you put in fresh bedding and wood shavings.

Treat your pets gently.

When you first take your pets home, they will be frightened. Leave them alone in their new home for a day and a night before you touch them. Then put your hand in the tank and let your pets smell your fingers. Talk gently so they come to know the sound of your voice.

Be very gentle when you pick up your pet mouse. Scoop it onto the palm of your hand. Never squeeze or hold it around the middle. Keep your pet away from your face.

Never pick up your rat or mouse by its tail. Always stroke them from the head to the tail.

To hold your pet rat, place a hand around its shoulders and support its hindquarters. Your rats will like being picked up and stroked. You should do this at least twice a day.

Help your pets stay healthy.

If your pet falls to the floor, pick it up gently and check to make sure it has no broken bones. Put it back in its home and do not touch it for at least a day and a night.

If it is not moving around as normal within 24 hours, take it to the vet.

If your pet gets plenty of exercise, its claws should not grow too long. Check the claws regularly. If they are too long, ask the vet to clip them for you.

If you do have to take your mouse or rat to the vet, make sure that it has plenty of its usual bedding to keep it warm.

Your pets should breathe easily without making a lot of noise. If your pets wheeze or sniffle, it is a good idea to take them to the vet.

Make sure your pets are safe.

You can leave your pets alone for one or two days. Check that they have enough dry food. Do not leave fresh food, since it will get stale.

If you are going away for longer than two days, ask a friend to look after your pets while you are away.

Make sure your pets have plenty of fresh water if you need to leave them for a day or two.

Mice usually live for two to three years, and rats for three or four years. If you care for them properly, they will have a happy life.

But, just like people, one day they will die. This will make you feel sad, but soon you will remember how much fun you had with your pets.

Words to Remember

albino An animal with white fur and pink eyes.

bedding Shredded paper you can buy from a pet store for use in your pet's nest.

litter A group of young born to a rat or mouse or other animal.

rodent The large group of animals that rats and mice belong to.

tank A glass container that can be used to house a rat or mouse. The lid should be close-fitting and allow plenty of air into the tank.

vet A doctor for animals.

whiskers Long, fine hairs that grow on an animal's face.

wood shavings Specially prepared shavings used on the floor of the cage or tank. Buy these from a pet store.

Rats grow quickly.

Newborn rats are tiny and hairless.

By 16 days a baby rat has a furry coat.

Index

bedding 13, 27

birth 10–11

cage 12

claws 27

cleaning 22–23

exercise 16–17

feeding 20–21, 28

holding 24–25, 26

play 17, 18–19

tank 12

teeth 15

vet 27

water 21, 28

Notes for Parents

Rats and mice will give you and your family great pleasure, but they do need care and attention. If you decide to buy rats or mice for your child, you will need to ensure that the animals are healthy, happy, and safe. You will also have to check that they have food and water, take care of them if they are sick, and help your child with the pets until he or she is at least seven years old. Rats and mice are ideal first pets, but make sure your child learns to handle the animals correctly and does not harm them.

Here are some other points to think about before you decide to own rats or mice:

- Mice live for two or three years, rats for up to four years, and will cost money to feed and house. If your pets become sick, there may be vet's bills.

- Do you have time to feed and clean your pets regularly and to play with them so that they do not get bored and lonely?

- Do you have other pets, such as dogs or cats, that might frighten the rodents?

- You need somewhere to keep the rats or mice indoors. A cage or tank for two or three mice should measure at least 20 x 10 x 10 inches. A cage for two rats should measure at least 30 x 25 x 10 inches.

- Pet rats and mice are usually good tempered. Remember, though, that they do have sharp teeth, and may bite if scared.

- It is best to have two rats or mice together. Two females will get along well, but two males may fight, even if they are brothers. Do not keep a male and female together. They will have unwanted babies.

- If you go on vacation, make sure someone can care for your pets while you are away.

This book is only an introduction for young readers. If you have any questions about how to look after your mouse or rat, you can contact the Humane Society of the U.S., 2100 L Street NW, Washington, DC 20037.